UTILITY

poems by

Joanne Ward

Finishing Line Press
Georgetown, Kentucky

UTILITY

Dear Ann & Stan,
Thanks so much for
your friendship all
these years!
Hope you like these,
Love,
Joanne

ACKNOWLEDGMENTS

Some of these poems have appeared in the following publications:

13th Moon—"Climbing" and "Substation"
High Voltage Women, by Ellie Belew, *Red Letter Press*—"The Trade
Experience"

Publisher: Leah Huete de Maines
Editor: Christen Kincaid
Cover Art: Margaret Shafer
Author Photo: Margaret Shafer
Cover Design: Elizabeth Maines McCleavy

Order online: www.finishinglinepress.com
also available on amazon.com

Author inquiries and mail orders:
Finishing Line Press
PO Box 1626
Georgetown, Kentucky 40324
USA

Table of Contents

I dedicate this book to my spouse,
Margaret Shafer,
with thanks and love

I

Climbing

1

When you're "weeny armed"
     and a woman,
the linemen who risk their lives every day
     on the poles
fifty feet up, or more,
say they've done their share of the dirty work
and fought their way to the top,

yell down
"If you can't hold the goddamn line
you'd better look for another job!"

And if you ask for help with a feeder arm
     going up, when you're new
     and sore and don't have
     meathooks yet for hands,

they'll jeer
"You gonna share your pay?
And how the hell did you pass the exam
     anyway, grunt?"

And all will ask how you like that
     little piece of meat that's walking by
     on the street,
and who do you sleep with, anyway?

2

We work on the ground,
scattered around the city.
We run our faces in the mud,
break our necks under the blistering sun,

watching, straining
to catch the new words that bounce
off the traffic, that are ground
through the saws and the drills and
         the hydraulics…
Good news! We sweat for our lives!
We are thirsty for whoever will shout
"You skin wire with your knife like this, you dummy.
This is number two and that's four;
measure with your arms and you can find
         more reels over there."

We watch the linemen climb,
slipping through the maze of wire.
They lean back on their hooks and their belts
as they cut and splice and
sweat out the hot connections,
swinging in the wind over the whole city,
balancing cross-arms and bugs and lamps
on their arms and legs
like acrobats
or mothers.

In a night sweat we dream
of swaying buckets
far above our heads,
the blinding sun behind them,
the mustachioed linemen
with the power in their hands
that can kill or save us all,
who tell us day after day
we're slow and stupid
cunts and bitches
who don't belong.

3

We come back to work each day.
Dirt-lined, slowly we gather
in the afternoon
before the last bell,
meet each other
in the underground locker room,
watch out for each other,
begin to notice the changes
as we turn to callous and leather
and move like our well-oiled tools,
hear how the cutting edges
of our tongues sharpen,
watch our arms turn to bare copper.

We climb. We push
and pull ourselves up the poles.
We begin to learn,
woman to woman, now,
and woman to man,
that taut ropes have always burned through
          our dreams,
and our muscles will hold.

Substation

Here is a yard full of power,
springs, switches, cooling towers.
Men raised it with their hands,
with their machines: the gears and levers
put together tooth in tooth,
wheel within wheel.

They pored over prints
of corners, trenches, walls;
dug holes, poured concrete pads,
rolled in the steel.
At the end of work they stay
for hours in the yard drinking beer
and lock the place of power in.

Woman comes here underground
as the female end—the hole end
in pipe fittings, knock-out punches, tampins.
Atop oil circuit-breakers
winds breeze through porcelain
skirts on the bushings.

Motors, generators, windings –
journeymen bend over them
intently, taking them apart,
turning parts in their hands,
calling them *mothers*,
imploring them to function.

Some women enter by decree.
One bursts out of the control building
shouldering number nine conductor wire.
She looks an oddity,
irritates like a stone
in the sock of old talk,
scares like a spy,

a moral fly in the ointment
of swearing that *the wife*
fills the lunchbox
always leaving something out,
cries, nags, pouts, has kids
and makes the bed to lie in.

Men bury women here,
who, like deer in the woods
above the mountain powerhouse,
wide-eyed, invisible as the night,
die of furious hearts,
die of fright
run to death.

1978—Affirmative Action in the Electrical Trade

Scene

I stand in a concrete alley that smells
of piss and garbage falling out of a dumpster.
Boxes of buildings fill with office workers
in the chilly morning, and I envy
their breakfast rolls and hot coffees.

The orange bucket truck sits tight
on its extended outriggers, its arms
unfolded and turned by hydraulics
the journeyman controls from above,
till the bucket sits next to the pole
and de-energized wires, where he can work
with hand tools or a chain saw or a come-along.

New to this job and unsure of my strength,
I grasp a half inch rope with gloved hands,
waiting for a tug, a yell, a signal from above
that a load tied to the other end of this hand line
on a pulley will get pushed over the edge of the bucket—
for me to stop its fall before It hits the ground.

Back Story

The lineman and I have to work together today.
He only knows I'm new, and a woman; I only
know he's big, with black hair and beard,
and he's been told to tell me what to do.
We're to dismantle the utility pole top down—
unload it of wire, insulators, cross arms and hardware...
He doesn't believe I can be of any help.
I know I'm not wanted.
The morning pitches us at each other.

Action

I stand still, the line in both hands,
almost leaning against it for comfort, while I
watch seagulls poke around in the garbage.
Suddenly, the line comes taut, comes
to life whipping upward through my palms,
barely leaving me enough time to see
the cross arm dropping on me.
I squeeze the rope, pull with all my weight,
stop the arm about ten feet in the air.
As I look up, the lineman stands behind
the edge of the bucket smirking.

Close-up

I feel shaky, my legs unhinged
like a puppet's with loose strings.
As I untie the cross arm from the hand line,
I'm struck by the blow of his silence,
what he didn't do—the ten foot long
four-by-four battering ram upended
out of the bucket with no word—
no battle cry announcing the war—
the first round of many I would win—some not,
to prove I was good enough to do "a man's job."

Still scared, I clench my fists, go on
with the job, as if nothing happened,
as if my heart weren't pounding my chest
like a drum roll announcing my spot on center stage.
I finish throwing the cross arms and the rest
of the salvage into a dump truck I'll drive
to the service center at the end of the day,
when I must find my way
to unload all the junk.

The Long View

The dirt of days-in and days-out
will collect under my nails and in the lines
of my hands, will cover my bruises, scars, other
near misses... Word will get passed on
to the crews, the utility, the city:
that we mean to stick it out.
Women will take and pass more tests,
will come, same as the men, to make a living.

Pinups

Female friends, like oracles, had warned me of pinups popping up in the cab of a truck, or on a bulletin board in the hall. I kept my head down, busy keeping track of all the tools I found myself using for the first time; trying to remember the tips about the easiest, most efficient ways to do things; trying to soothe my swollen hands before each day; hoping the men on my crew would see I was willing to work hard. Like an orphan with new parents, I kept my mouth shut, knowing that my affirmative action hiring, not to mention my sex, counted against me.

So when I was returning some wrenches to the transformer shop late one afternoon and passed by the bench room for battery maintenance, I wasn't expecting to see another woman there—buxom and bare, in spiked heels and on her back, a pinup almost three feet high on the wall—a giant *Playboy* fold-out for all to see in our own little museum of modern art! I admired her curves and complexion in brief, gawking—shocked at the size of the problem more than anything else.

The fellow in charge of batteries, George, was a quiet person, gray haired, tall, with a small paunch—not far from retiring. He didn't seem the type to have a three foot tall poster of a naked woman in his shop, but she had autographed her picture, "You're the best Georgie, xoxoxo, Angela".

I knew right away what to do. I found a *Playgirl* magazine with an oversized fold-out of a rugged guy with bulging muscles glistening in the photographer's light, his robust penis in plain sight. He was built for a comeuppance in the name of equal rights for women. After the work day was done, I waited for the security guard to come and go, and with the transformer shop dark, I slipped into the battery room, climbed up on the bench, quietly cut Angela down, and taped up my man, "Sam."

His poster was as tall as hers and even more commanding, because he was a "He," and had never shown off for the guys and gals at our service center. I signed, "Georgie, it's been great! Love, Sam," folded Angela under my jacket and beat it out of the building as fast as I could go.

I never heard word one about him. Sam was gone before the end of the next day. Nothing came down from high command. And no other naked women—or men—were ever pinned up there again.

Jim at Work

A tall, wiry journeyman,
mostly quiet on the crew,
he knew his business,
knew despite disgruntled men
with their stubborn backs up,
the time had come when he'd be told
to work with women.

He drove the oldest stick shift van,
too loud for us to say much on the way.
He was in charge of this job,
held the clearance to maintain
a 4KV air circuit breaker
in a metal-clad switchgear sub.

He liked a plan for how we'd go
about the work, what we'd do first,
who'd do what, the safety steps
we'd take, which tools he wanted me
to bring to the table in our makeshift tent.

With the dispatcher's go-ahead
he racked the breaker down
from its tight connection to the hot
copper bars above the roof,
and we rolled it from its cubicle
into the arc of our lamps,

a machine solid on its cart,
in a state of rest, dependent
on the first of routines I'd learn
over years for all makes and models,
as Jim led me through the way this breaker
opened and closed—its own invention
of levers, latches, rollers and coils,
its causes and effects.

He opened the manual's diagrams
for all the breaker's faces, built
to specs in the Nth. degree, full
of moveable parts that shined
in our light, that were designed
to work in instantaneous waves
he'd memorized over time.

This Journeyman was the first
to put a roller bearing in my hand
and choose to show me, step by step,
how to take it out, pull it apart,
clean and lubricate the races
and the balls—take part of a machine
apart—and put it back to work
within the whole as good as new.

In his view there was no reason
for me not to do this and more.

Notes:

"4KV air circuit breaker"—4 thousand volt air circuit breaker, or
ACB, which operates on the principle that an electrical arc caused
by the separation of energized contacts can be extinguished by air.

"metal-clad switchgear"—circuit breakers which are enclosed in
separate cubicles of a metal building, and whose main contacts
can be racked vertically to connect to electrical bus work running
horizontally above.

"sub"—substation: an enclosure of equipment used to reduce the
high voltage of electrical power transmission to that which will be
supplied to consumers.

The Trade Experience

*"The trade experience requires a strong sense of personal
responsibility. Tragedy is hovering over your shoulder always."*
—Matthew B. Crawford, Shop Class as Soulcraft

I wore a pair of new kid gloves
that didn't last a day
as the half inch hand line
burned through them,
up and down with the blocks,
the clamps, the come-alongs,
the wire, braces, lags,
the cross arms pushed off the edge
of the bucket high above—
whatever was cut away
dropped down on the line
for me to catch
before it hit the ground.

I was mum my first month,
wide-eyed, a breath of air
that had never seen a gale,
a candle that had never seen a ball
of white hot flame engulf the pole,
the bucket on the arm
of the Hi-Ranger, never saw
the lineman lose his arms,
the apprentice, caught on a macho crew,
climbing without a safety strap
around the pole, fall
and break her back.

I have a badge of honor scar
from a smashed thumb
in the bushing shop,
a screw driver tip melted
black from short circuits,

a bad back. I vowed:
On my honor I will wear
the yellow hard hat, steel toed boots.
I'll use the warning tape, the red flags,
rubber goods, the safety belts, the gloves,
the masks, the sweaty Tyvek suits.
I promise to obey the rules
for switching power off and on.

Fraternities of high jinks
carried long days
with jokes and insults
thrown across the bench,
excuses made for no hard hat
or sleeves rolled up on a hot day,
with taunts across the yard that meant
when the crew chief comes,
or when you make a stupid move
I'll watch your back.

We didn't want to see
the journeyman dead
from the untested line he grabbed
that flung him from the tower,
a silhouette against the sun,
plunging to the steel deck.

No longer before our eyes
in the substation, the mayhem
on a darkened basement wall
where the wireman smoldered
years ago, after he went to work
on a live breaker across the room
by mistake.

But over our shoulders always.

II

Utility

Electrical Helper

1
Coming off the street
it was enough at first
to coil and tie the half inch rope
in a figure eight,
to feel the socket fit
the bolt's hexagonal head,
the ratchet's click,
the purchase of steel
crescent wrench hands,
the heft of connectors
clamping over pipe
in small puzzles
of nuts and bolts and flats,
to learn how to snug copper
without stretching threads.

Stand a tall, wooden ladder up
like a tree, extend it rung by rung
forty feet into a jungle gym of steel,
clip yourself around a beam
in your climbing belt,
hanging back on your scare strap
to take apart and clean or build
with both hands at the same time.
Stand on your feet,
trust yourself to lean on air.

2
As if I were on the playground at school,
I could run the tools and hardware
up the hand line, keep ahead of the next step
and play marbles with the boys.

I could throw the wrench so well
that it would lift in slow mo,
lying on its side the whole way,
a gift that dropped lightly
in the journeyman's
upturned palm.

Crew

The electrical fields baked in August.
Sun bounced off the substation's fractured rock
        in a mirage of shimmering water.
The hair on the back of our arms rose from the yard's static charge
        as if it might escape swimming in skin.
We tied bandanas soaked in ice around our necks.

Late that afternoon we hoisted three breaker tanks and bolted them
        to flanges with air guns,
pumped the oil, gathered grunt bags with the tools, the rags,
        spare parts for the bins,
Dropped grounds from the grid and hefted them to the shed,
Agreed, each one, to sign away our clearance for the work done.

I headed to my truck for the drive home,
felt tingling on my neck to know that I was one of everyone
        who knew what job to do.

Career

I sat in the breakfast nook
at night reading text books,
class notes on how to read the prints,
manuals for the oil and gas and vacuum breakers,
with exploded drawings of the parts
unfolding past the end of the page,
with diagrams of how they worked,
the path of compressed air
through the chambers of a valve
that slammed the contacts closed
to launch power along the heavy lines
high above the streets.

I found the guys who knew I'd work,
who'd show me tips on how to pass
the transformer test,
who knew they could call me names
and I'd call them back,
who'd shut up when I raised my voice.
I had a chair at the lunch table.
The day I passed all the company steps
I thought I'd won a medal.
I walked to my locker in coveralls,
tool belt over my shoulder,
my throat full, then, for the balancing,
the scales ahead.

Transformer

We pick through
shattered crockery,
what looks like
transil oil at first,
all that's left
of the neighbor's cat,
a patch of hair
stuck to the steel
as if the transformer
had lived briefly,
spattered fat,
scorched paw prints
where a tabby stood
on its hind legs
and reached to the top
skirt of the bushing
to sniff the copper's
peculiar, hard blooms.

Scuffing our boots
in the gravel, we shake
our heads at the melting,
the burned copper
like the inner flesh
of a strawberry,
like metal bleeding.

Our foreman says
he's seen a cat
work its way
twenty feet up
or more
between a transformer's
cooling fins
like a rock climber.

Reluctant to gather
my tools for the day,
I half trace, half
imagine the path
of your supple spring
to the high garden,
the small field
of such interest,
that hums, that draws
you, without a thought
of what's next,
into a brilliant flash,
an early morning dance
where you turn to the world
outstretched, your transforming
blood, of a sudden,
steaming into air.

Apprentice

She wasn't a large girl
but really tough—
on the stubborn side—
Her mom had climbed
with the first women's team
to conquer Annapurna—
nearly died.

I saw her in the locker room,
a world unto herself,
as if she didn't believe
she'd been delivered
from a womb,
short but strong
on the pole in her hooks,
with good reports, we heard,
from the journeymen
who worked with her.

Proud to be one of the guys.
Trying to forget her sex
as she came through the gate
for the first time
with one, or two, or three,
to build a history on the dock
loading jeeps and bucket trucks
in the early a.m.
under all eyes:

in Carharts and leather
and shiny hard hat,
like a beacon exposing
the right of family,
that you had to have
a coat of arms
to be there—

meeting the barrage
of everyone who'd shout
at a woman what to do,
or the tight lips of anyone
who kept the secrets
about what to do.

I knew the day she'd find
that even the smallest guy,
even the brown or black man
who was just as new,
would learn the passwords
to qualify for the hood
ahead of her.
The closer she came
to her fourth year,
working high voltage hot,
the harder the diehards
would make it
not to disappear.

She didn't want to hear
woman talk,
no need to share
domestic, over-the-fence
recipes for wisdom,
what to watch out for,
who to get help from,
how she could fit in.
No amen corner for her.

Without generations
or drives or dreams alike
we shared only gender—
and those few women
who'd come before
through a chink
in the dam wall,

making their way
to the wired stations
and tunnels and streets
like a persistent
leak, and then a breach
that opens into a pool.

They could've told her
a reservoir of power
flows in the penstock
of women and men
who can open floodgates—

can vouch for you
when you ask,
vouchsafe to God Almighty
if need be, that you
can be good enough
to be a man, Amen!

Bitter Root

The water lies to the fish.
The soil lies to the trees.
The air lies to all of us
 who breathe.

The junkyard creeps into the woods,
brews like the bitter coffee
in our pot at work.
Today I bathe in transil oil.
Rubber and iron take root.

Animals

His hair hung to his shoulders,
a mane matted, uncut,
adorning nearly 300 lbs.
of muscle and belly,
jack-of-all-trades hands,
and the memory of an elephant.

He'd roar into work on his Harley
wearing that black helmet
that looked like a skull cap,
his blond hair flying out all sides
like the ruff of a lion.

He loved his mother, his old cars,
his body of appetites—
no regard for the management guys,
knew how to do his job
if he wasn't down flat with a hangover,
or just wasn't in the mood.

A big man to have on my crew,
bulldogging, bullshitting
his way through.

The day he and a buddy hoisted
a bushing to me and a Helper
10 ft. up on a circuit breaker,
we needed a delicate balance
of angle and speed to slip
the bottom of the bushing
into the tank of oil, matching
the bolt holes on each flange.

With an inch to go he let
his rope slip, dropped
the bushing hard and fast
on the steel, laughing
at our surprise.

Struck with missing
by a sliver smashed fingers
I rose up to a new beat
in a bullhorn, crew chief voice,
throwing my hat into the wild,
aiming my spit at his wide eyes.
"Rick, you fuckin' son-of-a-bitch,
don't you ever do that again!"

He shut up. Looked down.
Pulled his weight
when we started over.

Cable Terminations

Part of me misses the cable and wire now—
the concentric strands of copper, of aluminum
at the core. The strands that spiral along
wrapping tightly together to share their cargo,
electrons in an instantaneous rush
like the flush of a sudden laugh.

I remember the weight, the heft of it,
though I'm not strong enough to heft it anymore—
the broad coils and arcs of cable spooling
off hydraulic reels, filling tunnels or vaults
or breaker cable rooms, or expanses of air,
like copper suns or aluminum moons.

Always harder for smaller hands
to work it— unwieldy, exacting—
to pressure the cutters and strippers,
to turn the tools down and around
through the jackets, the semi-con, the shields,
the insulation. We took precise care
to slice only so far—to sand and clean
and cut and pare as if the dank tent
were a bright, dry kitchen.

Then crimping the connecter to the cable-end
with the proper die and press –
a squeeze down to the tightest fit
before slipping the heat shrink tubing
over the whole, and getting out the torch gun.
A dry seal without voids, in the end,
a bond that could withstand being connected
to the white hot power.

I didn't love to work with it.
I knew its layers could get the better of me,
would take another career in the downtown
underground network for us to bond.
Who knew I'd come to think of it now,
come to love the touch, the words of it?

Additional Acknowledgments

Special thanks to Clara Fraser, the iconic socialist feminist who took charge in 1973 of planning and implementing an affirmative action program for women at Seattle City Light, which resulted in the historic hire of the Utility's first ten female Electrical Trade Trainees, and without whom there wouldn't have been electrical trade jobs available for those of us who came and continue to come after.

Thanks, also, for the tenacity of those pioneering ETTs, who carried on through major obstacles to build successful and respected careers, while remaining dedicated to helping their co-workers navigate what often was a hostile work place, and for holding the City of Seattle and its publicly owned electrical utility accountable for the equal rights of working women.

My thanks to the Seattle group, the Greenwood Poets, for its members' steadfast friendship and support. Also thanks to the astute Vashon Island/Durland Ave. critiquers.

And a big thank you to my editor, Christen Kincaid, for all her help; thanks as well to the entire team of Finishing Line Press.

Joanne Ward was educated at Denison and Northwestern universities with a focus on theatre arts and the study of oral interpretation for her BA and MA. But after teaching briefly for the University of Illinois' Speech and Theatre Department, she focused on writing poetry and was accepted in the University of Washington's graduate creative writing program.

Over the next couple years she began publishing her work in literary magazines and journals, gravitated toward political activism, and became interested in non-traditional work for women, which was becoming more open to women and people of color via newly developed affirmative action programs. She landed a job as an electrical helper at Seattle City Light, one of a second wave of women hires, to forge her way, with the help of many others, for years to come.

Here she brings us a poetic memoir of her career in the electrical trade, as she worked in substation maintenance and construction. She tells us about working with her hands for the first time, illuminates the intricacies of large and complicated machinery, shares the pleasures and the challenges she faced working on crews dominated by men, and brings to life a utility that powers a great city's businesses and homes.

CPSIA information can be obtained
at www.ICGtesting.com
Printed in the USA
JSHW032026220221
11879JS00003B/19

9 781646 624188